DIRTY AND DANGEROUS JOBS

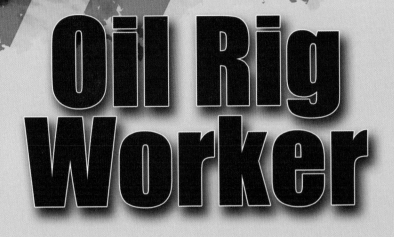

Oil Rig Worker

By William David Thomas

Reading Consultant: Susan Nations, M.Ed.,
Author/Literacy Coach/Consultant in Literacy Development

mc Marshall Cavendish
Benchmark
New York

Published by Marshall Cavendish Benchmark
An imprint of Marshall Cavendish Corporation

Other Marshall Cavendish Offices:
Marshall Cavendish International (Asia) Private Limited, 1 New Industrial Road, Singapore 536196 •
Marshall Cavendish International (Thailand) Co Ltd. 253 Asoke, 12th Flr, Sukhumvit 21 Road, Klongtoey
Nua, Wattana, Bangkok 10110, Thailand • Marshall Cavendish (Malaysia) Sdn Bhd, Times Subang, Lot 46,
Subang Hi-Tech Industrial Park, Batu Tiga, 40000 Shah Alam, Selangor Darul Ehsan, Malaysia

Marshall Cavendish is a trademark of Times Publishing Limited

All websites were available and accurate when this book was sent to press.

Library of Congress Cataloging-in-Publication Data
Thomas, William, 1947-
          Oil rig worker / by William David Thomas.
                p. cm. — (Dirty and dangerous jobs)
          Includes index.
          ISBN 978-1-60870-173-5
          1. Oil well drilling rigs—Juvenile literature. 2. Oil industry
          workers—Juvenile literature. 3. Petroleum workers—Juvenile literature.
          I. Title.
     TN871.5.T46 2011
     622'.3381—dc22   2009049821

Developed for Marshall Cavendish Benchmark by RJF Publishing LLC (www.RJFpublishing.com)
Editor: Jacqueline Laks Gorman
Design: Westgraphix LLC/Tammy West
Photo Research: Edward A. Thomas
Map Illustrator: Stefan Chabluk
Index: Nila Glikin

Cover: Oil rig workers on a drilling rig move part of the drill into place.

Printed in Malaysia (T).
135642

CONTENTS

Words defined in the glossary are in **bold** type
the first time they appear in the text.

Hard at Work

Bundled up against the cold, oil rig workers move a heavy drill into position. It is hard, dangerous work.

Andrew Pierce was working on an oil **rig** in Texas. He and some coworkers were replacing a broken part. What seemed like a safe, simple job nearly killed him.

The part, called a flange, was large and heavy. The new one had to be lifted into place by a crane. As the flange was being moved, it fell. It landed on top of Pierce, badly injuring him.

Danger: Hot, Wet, and Cold

Oil drilling rigs are dirty, dangerous places to work. They are found in the hot, dusty fields of Texas and the frozen ground of Alaska. Hundreds of them stand or float in the ocean, from California to the Gulf of Mexico. Every day, people on these rigs are injured. Some of them die.

What makes oil rigs so dangerous? Who works on them? If the work is so dangerous, why do they do it?

Roustabouts, Roughnecks, and Mud Men

The job of an oil rig crew is to drill holes in the rock to find oil. It isn't easy. Those holes may be thousands of yards or meters deep.

The lowest-level workers on a rig are called **roustabouts**. These are usually the newest or youngest men. They do a lot of cleaning because oil rigs are very dirty places. Roustabouts also carry tools and equipment from place to place.

Roughnecks are the next step up. They have been called the backbone of the oil

Dirt and oil cover everything on a drilling rig. Roustabouts like this one do some of the dirtiest work.

An Oil Drilling Rig

Oil rigs have lots of parts. Each one has a special job to do.

- The drilling floor is a large platform. Most work on a rig takes place there. On **offshore** rigs, the drilling floor rests on legs that go right to the ocean floor. Other offshore rigs, called **semi-submersibles**, actually float. They are held in place by huge anchors.

- The **rotary table** is a thick metal plate in the center of the drilling floor. The rotary table gets power from an engine to make it spin.

- A machine called a **kelly** locks into the rotary table and connects to the drill pipe.

- The drill pipe is connected to the drill bit. As the drill goes deeper, more sections of drill pipe are added.

- The drill bit does the actual work of cutting the rock. It may be as big as a person. It has wheels covered with sharp metal teeth. Together, the kelly, drill pipe, and drill bit are called the **drill stem**.

- The derrick is a tall metal frame. Thick steel **cables** called drilling line run from the top of the derrick to the kelly. These cables raise and lower the drill stem.

- As the hole is drilled, metal tubes or pipes called casing are placed inside. These tubes keep the hole from filling in.

- As the drill turns, "mud" is pumped into and out of the drill pipe. Mud is a mixture of clay, water, and several special chemicals. The mud helps to cool the drill bit. It also collects bits of drilled rock and carries them up to the surface. A machine called a shaker separates the rock from the mud. The bits of rock are checked for signs of oil. The mud then goes to a storage area called a pit.

- The blowout valve is at the top of the drill hole. It is an important safety feature. If oil is found, the blowout valve is closed to keep the oil from shooting out of the hole.

To see the parts of an oil rig, refer to the illustration on page 7.

industry. Roughnecks raise and lower the drill and use heavy tools to connect sections of drill pipe. They load and unload equipment, repair broken gear, and keep the mud pit filled. They may climb to the top of the derrick to fix cables.

Drillers and mud men are at the next level. The drillers are in charge of the drill bit. They give directions to roughnecks to install new drill pipe or casing. The mud men make sure the chemicals in the mud are mixed correctly. They also measure the amount of mud flowing in and out of the drill hole.

Tool Pushers, Crane Operators, and Cooks

The boss of an oil rig crew is called a **tool pusher**. He decides who works where and when. The tool pusher is

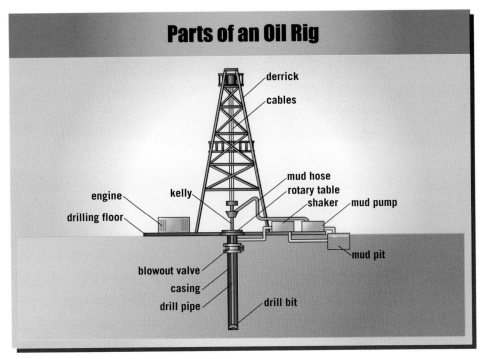

Parts of an Oil Rig

derrick
cables
mud hose
rotary table
engine
kelly
shaker
mud pump
drilling floor
mud pit
blowout valve
casing
drill pipe
drill bit

Drill bits are different sizes and shapes for drilling through different kinds of rock.

responsible for ordering supplies, keeping records, and making reports to the drilling company.

Every rig has a few specialists as well. The crane operator runs the big cranes. These machines move heavy loads of pipe and other materials around the work site. Oil rigs also have **welders** and electricians. Offshore rigs have divers and boat operators on board. Floating rigs have a specialist called a ballast man. His job is to make sure the

The derrick rises high above the ocean on this drilling rig. The large white platform on the right is a landing pad for helicopters.

rig stays as level as possible in the moving ocean. If the rig is not steady, drilling cannot go on.

Whether a rig is on land or sea, the crew needs food, coffee, and cold drinks. Cooks and dishwashers are part of the drilling team.

Drake's Folly

The first oil well in the United States was drilled in 1859, near Titusville, Pennsylvania. Edwin P. Drake was the drilling manager. People called the well Drake's Folly because they thought Drake was foolish. They were soon proven wrong. For many years, half of the world's oil came from Pennsylvania, which is sometimes called the Quaker State. Today, Drake's success is remembered in product names such as Quaker State Motor Oil and Pennzoil.

Edwin Drake (right) stands in front of his oil well, near Titusville, Pennsylvania.

Riding the basket to get onto an oil rig may look like fun. It can be very dangerous, however, when the wind is blowing and the waves are high.

Between 2002 and 2007, 598 oil workers died on the job. Hundreds more were injured. Peg Seminario is a safety official with a major **labor union**. She says, "This is a very, very hazardous industry with a very high rate of injuries and **fatalities**."

11

Weight and Waves

Why is working on oil rigs so dangerous? "There are a number of reasons," says Kim Bartlett. He once worked as a roughneck. "First, everything . . . weighs twice as much as it appears. . . . Because everything weighs so much, and because a large part of our job is moving objects around the rig, we depend on cranes to lift them. And once an object is in the air, even if only a few inches, it can drop on you."

For people who work on an offshore rig, just getting there can be dangerous. Helicopters usually carry workers to the rig. When the weather is bad, however, the helicopters can't fly. Workers then have to ride boats to

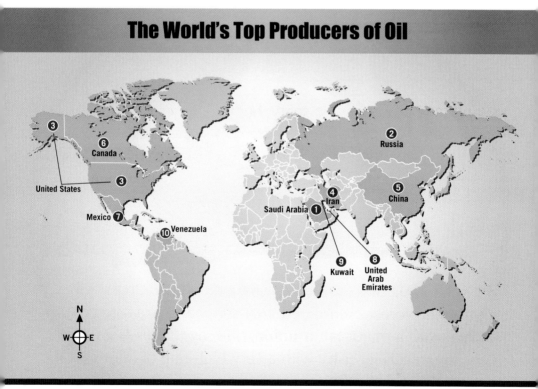

The World's Top Producers of Oil

3

6
Canada

United States

3

Mexico 7

10 Venezuela

2
Russia

4
Iran

5
China

Saudi Arabia 1

9
Kuwait

8
United
Arab
Emirates

N
W E
S

Thumpers

How do scientists decide where to drill for oil? One way is to use **vibrations**. Rock that holds oil vibrates differently from solid rock. To make the earth vibrate, huge trucks called thumpers slam heavy metal plates against the ground. (Sometimes, explosives are set off to make the earth vibrate.) Under the sea, blasts of compressed air are used to "thump" the ocean bottom. Scientists make careful records of the vibrations that thumping causes. They make drilling maps based on the vibration patterns. They use the maps to plan where to drill.

the oil rig. The trip can take four to eight hours, through waves that may be 15 feet (4.5 meters) high.

When the boat arrives, a few workers at a time climb into a woven rope "basket." A crane lifts the basket from the boat to the drilling floor. That can be a distance of 70 to 100 feet (21 to 30 meters). One worker said, "Nothing on the rig scares me more than the basket."

Fire

Riding the basket may be scary, but the biggest fear on an oil rig is fire. That's especially true for rigs in far-off places such as at sea or in Alaska. In those places, help may be hours away. Oil fires are hard to put out.

Natural gas is often found with oil. Natural gas can easily explode during the drilling process. Explosions can kill workers, destroy oil rigs, and start large fires.

Heat, Cold, and Hurricanes

Weather can make oil rig work even more dangerous. It can, in fact, be deadly. Julius Askew was a roustabout on a California oil rig. In May 2008, the temperature hit 103 degrees Fahrenheit (39 degrees Celsius). Askew collapsed

Red Adair: Hellfighter

When a rig catches fire, special teams are called in to handle the job. A Texan named Paul "Red" Adair (1915–2004) was famous among these specialists. He fought more than 2,000 oil fires on land and sea. One of them was a huge fire in Africa called the Devil's Cigarette Lighter. A movie was made about Red Adair's work on that fire. It was called *Hellfighters*.

Red Adair went to Kuwait, a country in the Middle East, in 1991. Adair led a crew putting out oil rig fires there.

from heat exhaustion. He died a few hours later. He was twenty-seven years old.

Oil drillers in Alaska don't worry about heat. They work outdoors where winter temperatures often reach 40 degrees below zero. **Frostbite** and **hypothermia** are constant dangers.

Summer and fall are hurricane season in the Gulf of Mexico. Hurricanes have strong winds and heavy rains.

Wind and waves pound an oil rig during a storm. Bad weather is one of the things that makes oil drilling so dangerous.

Bright yellow suits protect these oil rig workers from the rain. Working at night, and in bad weather, is just part of the job.

When these storms come near, thousands of workers must be taken off oil rigs by boat and helicopter. This is a very dangerous operation. It is much safer, however, than staying on a rig during a hurricane. In 2005, Hurricane Rita and Hurricane Katrina hit the Gulf within weeks of each other. Together, the two storms smashed more than 100 drilling rigs.

Twenty-Four/Seven

Work on an oil rig doesn't stop. It goes on 24 hours a day, seven days a week. A standard work shift is 12 hours. That is a long time for people who are doing hard, physically demanding work. Workers who are tired often make mistakes, which can be very hazardous. On an oil rig, even a small mistake can be dangerous. One roughneck said, "You're working right there in all that iron, you know. Things can happen if you don't keep your fingers in the right place."

Bad Decisions

Another danger on oil rigs has nothing to do with machinery or weather. The danger lies in bad decisions by workers. The misuse of drugs and alcohol causes many injuries and deaths on rigs each year.

Measuring Mud

Mud men on rigs carefully measure the mud going into and out of the drill pipe. If less mud comes out than goes in, it may mean the drill has hit a pocket of natural gas. The crew needs to be especially careful then, since even a small spark can make the gas explode or burn.

Two roughnecks, covered with dirt and oil, connect a new piece of pipe to the drill stem.

Working on an oil rig is a dirty job. Kim Bartlett, a former roughneck, talked about putting on his clean work clothes. He said, "They are 'oil rig clean' which means that any place else they would be considered filthy. The oil and mud has so **penetrated** the fibers that no amount of washing will ever make them presentable."

Lifeblood

If working on oil rigs is so hard, dangerous, and dirty, why do people do it? One reason is that the United States and most other countries need oil badly. Presidents, business leaders, and news reporters have said that oil is the lifeblood of the nation. Oil is needed to power cars, trucks, trains, and airplanes. The U.S. Army, Navy, and Air Force depend on oil to keep the nation safe. Oil heats homes. It is also used to make hundreds of products that are used every day. For some oil rig workers, keeping this "lifeblood" flowing is a big part of the job. They see their work as a contribution to the health, safety, and comfort of the people of the United States.

In many parts of Texas, Oklahoma, and Louisiana, oil is the lifeblood of entire towns. Often, there is not much

Disaster at Sea

The *Piper Alpha* was an oil drilling rig in the North Sea, off the coast of Scotland. In 1988, there was an explosion on the rig. It caught fire. Rescue helicopters were sent for the crew, but they could not land because of heat, flames, and strong winds. The pilots reported flames reaching 350 feet (107 meters) into the air. A total of 167 people died in the *Piper Alpha* fire. It was the worst disaster ever in offshore oil drilling.

other work. Many people work on the rigs or work to support those who do. One roughneck explained it. He said that in addition to the people working on the rig, "You've got welders, plumbers, electricians, and location builders . . . the truck drivers. . . . You got to haul the pipe, haul the mud, haul the rigs. It's a big network. . . . "

A ship brings supplies to a drilling rig at sea. Oil rig workers must help unload the supplies. Workers often ride these ships to and from the rigs as well.

Products from Oil

Oil is made into gasoline and airplane fuel. It is used to run power plants and provide heat. It is also needed to make many chemicals and different kinds of plastic. Here are some products made from oil:

artificial limbs	detergent	milk jugs
balloons	disposable diapers	paintbrushes
bicycle helmets	grocery bags	shampoo
candles	insect repellant	soda bottles
contact lenses	medicines	umbrellas

Big Money

A lot of oil rig workers put up with the long hours, the dirt, and the danger for one reason: money. People can earn a great deal of money working on oil rigs. Furthermore, the work does not require a college degree or a lot of training. Texas Richards manages his own oil company—in Texas, of course. He says, "We've got men out here with a fourth grade education earning $50,000 a year."

Donnie Lewis was a diesel mechanic in eastern Canada. He wanted to earn more money. He quit his job and went to work on an oil rig in northern Alberta, 2,000 miles (3,200 kilometers) from home. He doubled his pay. Lewis says, however, that it was the coldest, dirtiest job he ever had.

Advancement

Oil rigs do give workers a chance to move up. Nearly everyone starts out as a roustabout or roughneck. If they work hard and learn a lot, however, they can advance to a better job and earn even more money.

The ANWR Argument

In the 2008 presidential campaign, Barack Obama and John McCain argued about a piece of land in Alaska called the Arctic National Wildlife Refuge (ANWR). Business leaders, animal lovers, and hikers have argued about it, too. ANWR is home to millions of **caribou** and other animals. There may be a lot of oil under ANWR. Companies want to drill for the oil. They say the oil is needed. Other people want to block the drilling. They think oil drilling will ruin the environment. The argument is still going on.

A herd of caribou roams the Arctic National Wildlife Refuge, where there may be a lot of oil. People disagree about whether to drill for oil or protect the area and the animals that live there.

The control room on this ocean drilling rig is full of computers and other high-tech gear. Working here is cleaner and safer than working on the drilling platform.

J. C. Craft is one example of this. Years ago, he began working in the oil fields right after high school. Craft said, "I went from a roughneck to a driller, a driller to a tool pusher, a tool pusher to a superintendent, a superintendent to a manager."

Craft went on to become the president of Penrod Drilling, a company in Dallas, Texas. "It's a good life," said Craft. "Anytime you can start off as a roughneck and end up running an outfit . . . then you got a lot to be thankful for."

23

Not for the Timid or Shy

Workers struggle with a heavy piece of pipe on a drilling platform. Roughnecks need to be strong and able to work long hours.

A young man once learned an important lesson. His family was one of the richest in the United States. The family owned oil companies and much more. When the young man went into the oil business, however, he started at the bottom. He had to work hard, like many other young men. "I roughnecked a little. It's pretty hard work," he said. "I was young and dumb and thought I was strong, but I found out I wasn't all that strong."

Young and Strong

Very few oil rig workers come from rich families. Where do they come from? What kind of people are they? How do they learn to do the work?

As that rich young man learned, working on an oil rig is a job for the young and the strong. Heavy lifting, bending, pulling, and hauling go on all day long. For that reason, nearly all oil rig workers are men. Many women are not strong enough to do the work.

Most rig workers are young, too. One man who worked on an offshore rig was known as "grandpop" to the other people on the crew. He was only 47, but that was much older than everyone else.

Spindletop

In January 1901, Beaumont was a small town in southeast Texas. About 10,000 people lived there. Then drillers on a nearby hill called Spindletop found oil—a lot of oil. The oil sprayed so high that it could be seen 10 miles (16 kilometers) away. In one year, Beaumont grew to 50,000 people. It had more than 600 drilling companies and 285 oil wells. It was called a boomtown because it grew so fast.

An oil rig diver checks and tightens bolts on underwater pipes. It is dangerous work, but it helps keep everyone on the rig safe.

Lots of oil workers come from Texas and Oklahoma. Historically, that's where the most oil drilling was done. Roughnecks from there, and their sons, moved on to work in California, Alaska, and offshore.

The Oil Debate

The world uses a lot of oil. In the time it takes you to read this, the world will have used up more than 45,000 barrels of oil. About 1,000 barrels—that's 42,000 gallons, or 159,000 liters—are used every second!

The United States is the third-leading producer of oil in the world. It is also the world's top user of oil. The country uses about 20 million barrels of oil every day. To do so, the nation buys 15 million barrels of oil from other countries every day. Most people agree that the United States needs to stop buying so much foreign oil, but they disagree on how to do so. Some say that more wells should be drilled in Alaska and offshore. Others say that other sources of power—such as wind, solar, and nuclear power—should be used instead of some of the oil. The debate goes on.

Many people are also concerned about how long the world's supply of oil will last. They are afraid that in the future, there will not be enough oil to fill the need. Some people estimate that the world's supply of oil may run out in about 40 years.

Learning the Work

There are no classes or colleges that teach oil rig work. People learn it by getting a low-level job and getting on-the-job training. Kim Bartlett, who worked on an offshore rig, explains that "to do anything on an oil rig, you have to go roustabout first. . . . The reason is simple: after you have been a roustabout for a while, you have done everything, or at least seen how it is done. . . . Roustabouting is how you learn to do it."

Ships that Drill

Floating oil rigs are usually towed into place by tugboats. The oil rigs have powerful engines, however. The rigs can move on their own. For this reason, floating oil rigs are classified as ships by the U.S. Coast Guard. Floating oil rigs can travel at speeds of 4 to 5 miles (6.4 to 8 kilometers) per hour.

These Texas roughnecks (shown with the crew's dog, who is dirty, too) relax at the end of another day's work on an oil rig.

So You Want to Be an Oil Rig Worker

Being an oil rig worker is a tough job, and no schools or colleges teach it. It must be learned on the job. Oil rig workers need to be strong. They have to lift and move heavy objects all day long. The hours are very long. Workers must be able to keep going, even when they are tired.

Because it is dangerous and often done in isolated places, oil rig work pays very well. Beginning roustabouts can earn more than $40,000 a year. Experienced tool pushers may earn more than $100,000 a year. Trained welders, electricians, and scuba divers also can earn a lot of money working on an oil rig.

The job outlook for oil rig workers depends on the price of oil. When the price goes up, more workers are needed. When the price falls, oil rig workers may lose their jobs.

Rough and Rowdy

Oil rig workers are strong people who work hard. Most of them don't have a lot of education. On the job, they are often dirty. Their language may be rough, and their manners may not be the best.

One driller said, "If you're timid and shy, you'd better just stay out of the oilfield 'cause [oil rig work is] a rough, rowdy occupation."

Anchors Aweigh

Floating oil rigs have anchors to hold them in place in the sea. There is usually one anchor for each leg of the platform. Each anchor weighs about 30,000 pounds (13,600 kilograms).

The chains holding the anchors have huge, very heavy links. Each link is 18 inches (46 centimeters) long, and each one weighs 100 pounds (45 kilograms).

cable: A kind of rope, often made of twisted metal.

caribou: A large animal in the deer family.

drill stem: On an oil rig, the kelly, drill pipe, and drill bit together.

fatality: Death caused by an accident or violent act.

frostbite: A serious injury to parts of the body, such as the fingers or ears, caused by extreme cold.

hypothermia: A very low body temperature, which can cause death.

kelly: On an oil rig, a machine that goes through the rotary table and connects to the top of the drill pipe.

labor union: An organized group of workers.

offshore: Away from land; in the ocean.

penetrated: Gone into or passed through something.

rig: A large platform used as a base for drilling for oil; also refers to the drilling floor, its supports, and everything on it.

rotary table: On an oil rig, a heavy metal plate powered by an engine that spins the drill pipe to turn the drill.

roughneck: A worker on an oil rig who handles tools, pipe, and other materials.

roustabout: The newest, lowest-level worker on an oil rig.

semi-submersible: A type of rig that is partly floating and partly under water.

tool pusher: The boss on an oil rig.

vibration: A fast movement that goes back and forth or up and down.

welder: A worker who uses burning gas or electricity to melt and join together pieces of metal.

BOOKS

Farndon, John. *Oil*. New York: Dorling Kindersley, 2007.

Gunderson, Cory. *The Need for Oil*. Edina, MN: ABDO Publishing, 2004.

Horn, Geoffrey M. *Oil Rig Roughneck*. Milwaukee: Gareth Stevens, 2008.

Manatt, Kathleen G. *Searching for Oil*. Ann Arbor, MI: Cherry Lake Publishing, 2007.

McCage, Crystal. *Oil*. Farmington Hills, MI: Greenhaven Press, 2006.

Parks, Peggy J. *Oil Spills*. Farmington Hills, MI: KidHaven Press, 2005.

WEBSITES

http://www.conservation.ca.gov/dog/kids_teachers/Pages/Kids%20and%20Educators.aspx
Click on photos and drawings to learn about the parts of oil wells, drilling rigs, and offshore platforms. Read a comic book about oil exploration in California.

http://www.howstuffworks.com/oil-drilling.htm
Learn more about how scientists find oil, how it is drilled, and how it is refined. Check out video clips and photos of oil rigs at work.

http://tonto.eia.doe.gov/kids/energy.cfm?page=oil_home-basics
All about oil, including how it is formed and produced.

Page numbers in **bold** type are for photos, maps, and illustrations.

About the Author William David Thomas has written books for children and young adults, software documentation, training programs, annual reports, a few poems, and lots of letters. He likes to go backpacking and canoeing, play his guitar, and watch baseball. He is the author of *Korean Americans* in Marshall Cavendish Benchmark's *New Americans* series, as well as several other books in the *Dirty and Dangerous Jobs* series. He lives in Rochester, New York.